Possum Nocturne

I0884705

Also by Doug Ramspeck

Black Tupelo Country
Where We Come From

Possum Nocturne

poems by

Doug Ramspeck

NorthShore Press

Copyright ©2010 by Doug Ramspeck
All rights reserved
Printed in the United States of America

NorthShore Press
717 Brown's Landing
Port Alsworth, AK 99653
northshorepressalaska.com

Distributed by
The University of Akron Press
Akron, OH 44325-1703

Author Photo: Michael Ayers
Cover Photo: Steve Kahn
Layout and Cover Design: Anne Coray
Logo: Greg Solomon

Library of Congress Control Number
2010934067

Ramspeck, Doug.
Possum Nocturne / by Doug Ramspeck.
ISBN-10: 0-9794365-3-2
ISBN-13: 978-0-9794365-3-6

This book is printed on 50% recycled paper.
Layout was accomplished with the use of photovoltaic power.

For Beth and Lee. And in memory of Audrey Ramspeck.

Acknowledgments

Grateful acknowledgment is made to the editors of the following publications where the poems in this collection were originally published:

The Briar Cliff Review: "Carapace"
The Chaffin Journal: "Bottomlands Death"
Chautauqua Literary Journal: "Mud Voice"
Cider Press Review: "Ghost Memory," and "Sumac Prophecy"
Confrontation Magazine: "Tattoo"
Connecticut Review: "Alluvium"
The Cortland Review: "Unmoored"
DMQ Review: "One Hundred Trains"
Ellipsis: "Bottomlands Rapture"
Hawai'i Pacific Review: "Driving on the Ridge and Seeing Smoke"
Hayden's Ferry Review: "Salt"
Hunger Mountain: "Horizon"
Iron Horse and *Verse Daily:* "Possum Nocturne"
New Delta Review: "Extremity"
New Zoo Poetry Review and *Verse Daily*: "Late Husband"
Nimrod: "Field Guide at Noon"
Northwest Review: "Black Tar Morning"
Passages North: "Equivalence"
The Pinch: "Wooing"
Poems & Plays: "Early Snow," "The Myth of Regeneration," and "Swamp Dance"
Prairie Schooner: "Swamp Blossoms"
Rattle: "Gift Skull"
Rhino: "Raising the Dust" (as "Mud in Heaven")
River Oak Review: "Archaic Light" and "Bitter Duration"
San Pedro River Review: "Field Guide in Winter"
Sentence: "Ladder Without Rungs"
South Dakota Review: "Prefigured"
Southern Humanities Review: "Residue"
Sou'wester Review: "Gargoyle"
The Spoon River Poetry Review: "The Art of Woods" "Embrace," and "Forsaken"
Story South: "Fifty Teeth"
Subtropics: "Field Guide in Snow"
Tar River Poetry: "Dun-Colored Photograph"
Third Coast: "Feral Evening"
Valparaiso Poetry Review: "Bright Snake"
Weber—The Contemporary West: "After the Storm," "Ghost Child," "Old Country," and "Vespers"
West Branch: "Divining Elegy"
Willow Review: "Swamp Lines"
Xavier Review: "Marsh"
Yalobusha Review: "Accustomed Hour"

"After the Storm" and "Ghost Child" were selected for the 2009-2010 Sherwin Howard Poetry Award by *Weber—The Contemporary West.*
"The Art of Woods" was selected by *Spoon River Poetry Review* for a 2008 Editor's Prize: First Runner Up.
"Carapace" was nominated by *The Briar Cliff Review* for a Pushcart Prize.
"One Hundred Trains" was nominated by *DMQ Review* for a Pushcart Prize.

Contents

Gift Skull 3
Swamp Blossoms 4
Old Country 5
Equivalence 6
Horizon 7
Raising the Dust 8
Marsh 9
Feral Evening 10
The Myth of Regeneration 11
Field Guide in Snow 12
Dun-Colored Photograph 13
Early Snow 14
Gargoyle 15
Unmoored 16
Salt 17
Bottomlands Rapture 18
After the Storm 19
Ghost Child 20
Embrace 21
One-Hundred Trains 22
Divining Elegy 23
Ghost Memory 24
Tattoo 25
Fifty Teeth 26
Sumac Prophecy 27
Extremity 28
Field Guide at Noon 29
Residue 30
The Art of Woods 31
Swamp Dance 33
Archaic Light 34
Bottomlands Death 35
Black Tar Morning 36
Mud Voice 37
Alluvium 38
Late Husband 39
Bitter Duration 40
Accustomed Hour 41

Driving on the Ridge and Seeing Smoke 42
Forsaken 43
Wooing 44
Bright Snake 45
Swamp Lines 46
Vespers 47
Prefigured 48
Field Guide in Winter 49
Ladder Without Rungs 50
Carapace 51
Possum Nocturne 52

Gift Skull

For years she kept it hanging like a mute wind chime
from a sweetgum limb near her tomato plants.
A bleached possum skull she'd discovered
with her fingers while planting seeds. *The dead mother us*,
she thinks each time she sees it, as though we suckle
at the open eye socket, as though fifty teeth are the only
comfort we can know. Once she watched a marsh hawk
struck by a pickup while it was swooping low across the road.
The bird lived for a few moments in the drainage ditch:
twitching like an epileptic, gathering itself in the great shroud
of wings. Sometimes the wind sways the skull as though the ghost
in it has come alive. She might be watching from the window
or kneeling before her vines, and the gift of the moving skull
reminds her of rocking a child in a cradle, reminds her
of gripping her knees and rolling forward then backward
and then weeping. After her infant son died, her breasts
were still heavy and swollen with milk. She imagined
it as ghost milk. And after the hawk grew still, she stood
at the side of the road and thought of the possum
waddling once out of the woods and now swaying
as a skull on a string, the wind rolling through its open
eye sockets and along the great profusion of its teeth.

Swamp Blossoms

Here is the watery grave. We are not
slave to it. This is not forever.
The ghost of stone lifting as statuary
in the old field beside the sleeping lake.
How pale the sky appears.
The skin of it representing itself as light.
Blossoming and calling and calling.
And from these shallow waters
the yellow flag and pickerelweed
and water lilies aflame
with summer. This is what it means
to cry out like peeper frogs and chorus frogs.
What it means to be a cottonmouth
slipping like ripe fruit into the lake.
How maligned the night is: the old skull of moon blooming
like bone amid the swamp.
While the young lovers are slipping down
to the earth, offering their naked skin
and blood to the mosquitoes.
Anointed in starlight. The ash of water
congealing into mud. Surely a child
will be formed in the young woman's belly.
And then the rains will fall. Stirring the waters
into foam. Washing the body. Then later
the child will be born in the cabin
by the lake. The blood blossoming
on the bed sheets. We are not slave to it.
The plosives of wings outside the window
as the cranes and egrets take flight.

Old Country

The old men are talking about a mule deer.
They believe it is a ghost. They believe
that the half-moon prints gouging the earth
near the drying stream were made long before
the ground hardened into stone, before the rains
stopped and the sky turned dry as salt.
There are days when the sun reminds them
of a tongue listing mute and swollen in a mouth,
when they stand on their back porches or walk
amid the rabbitbrush and imagine the landscape
around them as a desiccated tooth, as a severed
limb, as a forgotten country of cracked earth
and dead skies. A common story in these parts
is of a deer that was shot in the neck
and so transformed itself into a prickly pear.
Other mule deer arrived to feed on the body,
to drink the blood. And in the moonlight
those new ghost deer would wander out into
the sagebrush. No human eye could any longer
see them. Still they left their hoof prints in the earth.
And each time an old man knelt to touch the grooves,
the land around him would harden into stone.

Equivalence

It isn't simply the whispering
of leaves, the gray owl separating
itself as an occultation from the gray limb.
It is the equivalence of things:
clouds slinking above the bottomlands
as warnings, moonlight undulating as spirit
in the sleeping pond. One noon
she is stung on the eyelid by a vespid wasp.
She gathers larkspur and hound's tongue.
Mixes them with cow's milk and butter
into a salve. It is the smell
of loam in the dead of summer
along the river bank. It is the dirt
smeared like dried blood on a magnolia limb.
She sees it clearly:
the owl is the vespid wasp is
the hound's tongue is the gray limb
is the occultation is the sticky
paste clinging to her eyelid.

Horizon

For all these years I've held my tongue—
but tonight a pale violet light from town
haunts this low-slung sky above the cistern.
And this far out, beneath the prairie dark,
these country roads trail flat and unremembered.
Land stares at you. Wind washes
through the corn like air collapsing
in a lung. The spirit can't abide.
This is the myth of distances.
And this very dusk I stood amid
the motherwort and sweet-joe-
pye-weed and watched a red-tailed
hawk skim low across the field
behind the barn—skim and skim
until I knew there was no hope.

Raising the Dust

The mud in heaven must grow thick
with flies in summer. Celestial flies
that lift themselves above the tall
stink of grass. And what clings
to the bottoms of my father's boots
is holy as pig manure, damp and alluvial,
tracked into our mother's kitchen. And so
the smell of ammonia in the air, the sloshing
sounds from the bucket my brother carries
two-handed from the sink. Always the mud
and dirt that find their way into the house—
field mud congealed with bits of stone
and hay and grass. Loose earth collecting
in windowsills and stairs, dust seeping
from bookshelves and overhead fans,
handprints smudging countertops and walls.
Everywhere grime gathering like the leaf
meal beneath our oak trees beside the barn,
the trees that empty themselves each fall
until they are bare skeletons, that make
of the earth their own dark decay.
And so our father's body, that fine salt of dirt,
unneeded now, loam that once was drawn
from the earth to make a man. It was in
our back field where we found him,
face down in the mud, a hand clutching
his chest. He must have climbed from
his tractor and made his way as far as the fence.
While our mother, not yet knowing, on
her knees in the kitchen, leaned her weight
into a blue sponge to make the floor shine.

Marsh

The fish are smaller than I remember,
Most no larger than a finger. And the marsh
waters more shallow, as though the years
of sunlight have worn them away. I imagine memory
waiting in the cattails, as though it is what captures
the reeds and makes them sway, not all in one direction
but swirling, the way you might stir a pot.
These swamp candles are the same bright yellow
I remember, with the same drop of blood at the center,
the sky insignificant at last, as though the years
have tamed it. There is a fence we used to sit on
in the evenings, and once we saw a sandhill crane
leaping comically in the air in courtship. There is
a monotony to longing, as though the sun fills a body
until it floats away, as though you might sit
by the water's edge and that will be a life.
At times it seems that there is nothing left
but these reeds in the wind. We judge an hour by its
proximity to longing. When love comes to an end,
we think of the moon impaled in the trees
at midnight, bleeding white on the water.
And of the ghosts that rise from the lake
and make their way into the sky.

Feral Evening

Not the bats diving
out of the junipers and birches. Not
the sun impaled and bloodied
at the field edge.

Just this old woman
kneeling by a dead crow.

In another life this bird was made
of mud. Dense mud, dream mud.
Maybe it rose from the stale bottom
of a deep pond. Was birthed
beneath a yellow moon.

Or perhaps a pine snake
came whipping out of the fireweed
and loosed its skin. So was there no body?

Imagine a crow lifting a snake skin
and flying above the milkweed
and lamb's quarter.
Or a crow and snake
as witchery and necromancy.
A crow raising the dead flesh.

Surely the old woman
dreamed that this was so.

And then: What's this?
She is kneeling before the stain
at the field's verge. The black feathers
in the wind's path.

Look: even in death the wings ripple
and twitch as though alive.

The Myth of Regeneration

An unwelcome task, this business
of prowling in her garden after sunset,
burying beneath her tomato plants
a four-toed salamander wrapped around
a slender lock of hair. Here is the mad dance,
the feast of four directions. Here is the sacrifice
that fevers into vision then burns the eye
so all that's left are the skeletal limbs
of the trees beyond the field.
What has cleaved from her is slick as mud,
disfigured as submerged rock at the pond bottom,
weightless as the cursed root. Two summers earlier
splashing rain summoned Septoria blight
and turned her tomato leaves brown.
No amount of watering or pruning called them
back. What contracts and breathes inside her lungs
is atrophy itself, mummified tomato,
stink and permanence of dead flesh.
And so the blood that flows nightly in her veins
thrums like a tide as she kneels in the dirt, as the swollen
moon shines pale as bone above her maples.

Field Guide in Snow

The moon must have broken into pieces
and is ashing down,
                    great clumps battering the tall grass.
While the creek is sliding black
into the night's throat,
                                        swallowing.
This is the problem of winter,
the ground that hardens
into stone,
                    the heart with its skin
of ice, as though we have come to this
out of our own eyes,
                              the cornea and sclera
protecting us,
                              as though nothing
should ever reach us raw.
And what of the *I, I, I* forever throbbing
in our thoughts
                like a lit fuse, sputtering?
Or this snow that collects on our shoulders,
in our hair, cold as the moon,
                    this prophecy of
                                            shattering?
And the old gnaw in the belly,
the fog that will levitate
at first light
                    from the snow and grass,
the souls and their reluctance
to be gone from us, this clinging
                                        to dumb substance.
Like the morning I came across
                smears of blood
where a deer
                          must have been dragged
by the hunters, a path of red trailing
the fresh snow.

Dun-Colored Photograph

The blackjack oak droops
its severed limb into the river.

And though that limb has died,
it still sprouts its summer greenery.
And behind that tree, half-hidden,

there is a dun-colored horse,
and, behind it, an open eye of field,
which is another way of saying

something is missing.

Aristotle believed that the eye
sends out mysterious emissions
to make the world visible. To make
the blackjack oak visible.

But poor shutter eye: it cannot tell
the limb is dead.

Still, I know the field.
This very moment I am walking into it.
The dun-colored horse is accepting

an apple from my palm.

Early Snow

It has come to this again,
the uncertainty of memory,
deer tracks appearing
along the river bank
as twin half-moons,
cleaving into the mud.
Or the lightning that felled
the hickory limb
outside his bedroom window
when he was nine.
Or the time he followed
his wife into the woods,
where she picked cinquefoil
then abandoned the flowers
across a fallen, moldering log.
Once in a late October snowfall
he saw a dead doe
half-buried in the river's mud.
The moving water
blessed her. The moving
water anointed her.
The scooped weight of memory
washing across
the hollowed fur.

Gargoyle

There were warnings. The apples in the orchard
were decaying. You could smell them through
the screen mesh. And the truth was that insects swarmed,

rising from the bittersweet and goat's rue, rising
like strange words stammered from a dead tongue.
Sometimes the wind carried musky scents from the lowlands,

and my brother and I were drawn into the elms
and hickories. This was the oldest part of the woods
where once we found a dead wild turkey half hidden

in the leaf meal. Another time a possum skull posed as a gargoyle
by a moccasin flower. The words my brother spoke
were moans and grunts and also a strange whistle that escaped

from the fleshy back of his throat. His real voice was
the hoot owl, I imagined, or the fireweed clawing
through the charred earth after a great, cleansing blaze.

The wild turkey we found couldn't seem to tell
itself from mud, and in my dreams my brother's tongue
was impaled on a barbed-wire fence or floated

as murky green muck on the surface of our pond.
One morning I was kneeling there with my brother
when some minnows were attacked by a small-mouthed bass.

There was a great thrashing like something either dying
or attempting to be born, and my brother waded out
from ankles to knees to waist, as though

to follow the bass into the depths, as though he too
had been swallowed, as though the minnow were a tongue,
as though that tongue could speak only in the belly of a fish.

Unmoored

The powdered remains
of the moon are falling
like snow beyond
the loblolly pines.

The widower is dreaming this.
The snow covering the field
like a discarded snake skin

that disintegrates in your fingers,
as though the snake
is attempting to reassemble itself
in the field.

Or he is dreaming that someone
is coming toward him—
the black hair unmoored
in the night sky—
while he is walking through
the snow blowing
like mystery beside the river.

Salt

She wanted a son.
Wanted to gather epidendrum. To make of them a garland.
To preserve them in a jar beside her bed.
Then there was the matter of the crow. She found it
decomposing beneath a river birch near the swamp.
Wanted to bury it with its orange eyes still open.
Wrap its body in a discarded cottonmouth skin.
Grip a single feather in her fist when she gave birth.

Her father lost
two fingers in an accident. Kept them for years inside
a pickle jar. He would shake the jar
and watch the fingers float and list inside the formalin.
When he died she imagined him calling to her.
Screeching to her like a barred owl.
As though the tricholomas
growing from the conifer stumps were fingers.

When she married
she ground up click beetles and snout beetles
and vespid wasps to sprinkle in her husband's pockets.
His skin appeared sickly in winter. The moon
resembled salt above the cypress swamp.

When her son
was born she petitioned the Spanish moss and pickerelweed.
Threw the crow feather into the congealing waters.
Summoned the alligator snapping turtle from the depths.
In her dreams it carried severed fingers
like children in its belly.

Bottomlands Rapture

They say there was fire here once. And then the bald cypresses appeared. Stuck their knobby knees up through the brackish waters. Made a specter of moonlight. Walked with the purple gallinules on the lily pads.

My brother's asthma is a form of longing. The ache to draw fetid air into the lungs. The rasping rapture, tortured as boots slurping through wet mud.

At night I hear him summoning air. He makes of the effort an apparition. Wind squeezing through the narrow opening of a window jamb. Whistling at a window jamb. The ghost dance as labored provenance.

The vultures circling as we go swimming in the lake. An alligator snapping turtle rising to the surface. The green muck clinging to the carapace. The green muck clinging to our skin.

Each new breath divines itself, devours itself. Like lungs hardening into stone. The old fire of it. Like moonlight illuminating the outstretched and supplicated arms of the willow oaks. You lean into it. You close your eyes. You draw in each new searing breath as prayer.

After the Storm

And so she rises. Crosses
to the window. Looks out into
the lowlands.
                    Or let's say that in her dream
a massasauga, small as a dropped twig,
injects alluvial venom
                                        into her blood.
The lightning stitching its way
into the night sky. Impaling
the night sky. The rain
                              falling like a hanged man
then spreading out as a
                                        dark slough.
The poor snake drowning in the current.
The awakened woman rising from her bed
and gripping two hands
                              beneath her belly.
Carrying her swollen belly.
                    While the low earth is wet
and black with mud.

Ghost Child

As if the sweetgum trees leaning
toward the slough were whispering.
As if the muddy waters knew to speak.

She walks into the alluvium of morning:
daylight depositing its fertile light
atop the leaves. Let's say this is a wet
grave:

some child slipping beneath the water lilies.
Some child sinking beneath
the flowering wapato.

And since the slough is sickly and congealed—
the way a body grows thick and swollen
at the belly, the way a body rots
then ferments—

she imagines fish and frogs swimming forever
beyond vision, whole lives twisting and lost
in the slow mire.
The mud life, she imagines:
the ghost child fouled and abandoned,
in the murky waters of the slough,

the smell of it

like something dragged and dripping
from the dark loam.

Embrace

Tea from the staghorn sumac
simmers on the stove. It must be childhood
again: the flesh of morning steeping
in the open field, blessing the open field.
The wind carried through the long grass
to rattle at the kitchen screen: tambourine summer,
the dark eyeballs of the Virginia creeper
watching from the garden verge, my mother
placing the filled cup before my father—

as though any memory might crawl up
from the river like a stray dog: ribs distended,
nose groveling at the pokeweed and brambles,
the ambled gait as erratic as my father
weaving up from the barn to urinate
on the tomato vines. Then, later: the tomatoes
plopped on our window sill like malformed hearts.
Ungreening. Conjuring themselves as blood.

As though any memory might become as pleated
as the fireweed themselves, which, when the seedpods
open, reveal the cloud down; or the dog licking
at my father's pants after he went out,
as though any cloth might be a sustenance,
as though a .22 pistol touched to the skull
is a merciful embrace—the dog's ribs
embracing flesh—

or the sweetness of this honeyed tea
against a tongue. *Blessing the field. Blessing*
the tambourine summer. Washing over the tomatoes on our sill.
This wind playing its small instrument upon us.

One Hundred Trains

The power went out in our house
when I was nine, and for four days
winter found us. The ice storm
coated the maple trees in pure
cocoons of ice. The fallen limbs
were strewn like bones. My father
built a great fire from which the heat
hollowed us, scooped us out, then filled
us. That summer my brother and I caught
bullfrog tadpoles the size of sparrows
in the fetid pond. Nothing lasts. The sky
opens and the rain leaves pockmarks
in the water. The trains lift along the ridge
then disappear. Later my father admitted
how every train was a temptation—
to climb aboard, to lie on the tracks.
Later I would drive by the house and imagine
myself beyond the upstairs window
beneath the chimney. Sometimes my brother
and I would take off our caps at dusk
then throw them in the air so bats
would chase them, or we would walk along
the ridge to watch the trains. They roared
over the river and hollowed out our bones.

Divining Elegy

Toward the milkweed and oxeye daisies
she aims her sight. At the field's edge
the line divides between transparency
and mystery. Something hides
in the junipers and quaking aspens.
As a child she imagined death as light
elongating itself beyond the railroad tracks
at dusk, lying down on the horizon
like orange fire. Her youngest daughter
walked that morning for the first time.
Lifted herself. Wobbled for an instant
like an occultation. This evening the ground is wet
with weeping from the day's rain. The stream
is swollen and muddy. The bass that swim
there sometimes follow the minnows
into the shallows then strike.
Dark descends and the loblolly pines
are gray smudges against the prophecy of sky.
The limbs of the cherries spread out
like broken vessels. When she gave birth
she felt as though her body were burning.
She felt broken as stone. Her daughter lifted
herself as though she were the first creature
dragging herself from all fours.
Something was coming. Something
could almost be foretold.

Ghost Memory

I am six, I think, and I have turned away
and am squinting up the great road
where sunlight ghosts—thresholds
at the lake's edge. Think of stains,
of a sepulchral red dimming like fine dust
on the exposed loam. It hasn't rained
for weeks, but now I see dusk clouds
gathering beyond the birches where the dirt
narrows and leads up into the hills.
It does no good to imagine climbing there,
as though the horses I saw once on the ridge
are real—they aren't—if by real we mean
attainable; and I have turned away because
the last life of the yellow perch I dragged
onto the dock is writhing out of it.
I can't breathe. I remember a voice
following me, which is another way
of saying that the cattails—some exiled
beyond where the water has retreated—
have become for me translators of the wind,
which whispers of the wall of rain I see
veiling past the birches. In a moment
the drops will strike as pockmarks in the lake,
and the perch will dance then die against it.

Tattoo

Because
the slash pine toppled in the rain and grazed the house,
she imagines the body giving way,
the earth dampening and weakening like decaying gums.
There are no origins here: just the sky, a darkening
tattoo above the oaks, and more rain falling,
puddles forming as auguries in the lowlands.
In her dreams at night the mosquitoes slip
through the wire mesh and make of her blood
a congealing river, or a white-tailed deer gives birth
to a fawn in the saw-palmetto, the rain anointing
the newborn into swamp. All day she hears drops dripping
from the eaves, as though life is leakage and fluid
and spit. Often she rubs the ointment into her belly and her breasts,
and she imagines the river rising
from the darkness and overflowing its banks,
every pine tree in the woods losing its grip
and being carried off in the gathering flood of liquid mud
pouring out of the lowlands to find her.

Fifty Teeth

Once, as a child, she found in the woods beyond the stream,
half buried in the soft mud by the forget-me-nots,
a possum skull: rounded as a moon after the sludge
was fingered and thumbed away, pasty as insect larvae
feeding on dead flesh: the fifty teeth locked in the death grimace.
Of course the skull engendered her worst dreams:
a small bird trapped and writhing in an open eye socket,
claws searing at her back flesh then tearing in.

Yet often she fell asleep stroking the smooth skull on her chest
like a purring cat, or probing a finger along every ridge
and slice of sharpened bone, whispering into what once had been
an ear. She imagined the possum laboring out of the woods
into light as dense as the fog that formed some evenings
at the stream's base then drifted upwards into something
inconsolable, one more sorrow scaling the mountain
on tired legs. Light so cold it clung to her pale skin.

Sumac Prophecy

She was a child when the hawk came down.
Its mottled wings like those of a giant moth.
But she did not think it was a moth
or hawk—she thought a tear had opened
in the seam of things, that the sumac tree
at the field edge had displayed its hairy seeds
so let into the world a great and violent fluttering.
Later she would recall the apparition's
blood-red tail against the apparition's
blood-red seeds, as though a divination
had unfolded itself out of drowsy sunlight
in a Michigan field, as though what had arrived
would lift her on its talon hooks until the world
diminished as small as a future gray morning
when she awoke to great stabs of pain
and blood-red thighs and remembered
the apparition scattering robin feathers
then lifting dead flesh to carry it away.

Extremity

Say it is the orchard at first freeze. The morning vapor a white tongue swollen and heavy against the earth. Soon there is a narrowing of vision, the stilled canals between the apple trees that yesterday were overflowing in a downpour.

Or a red fox we see eating decaying apples in the snow. The daytime sky stagnant. The apples fermented, the smell of them strong, even in the cold. Or suddenly a jay calling out as though in warning from above. The fox looks up. My brother and I look up. Our necks strain.

Or say it is our father like Saint Sebastian wandering in the orchard in a late-season storm, entreating the sky. Imploring the sky to spare us the deep freeze. Begging the sky to be a cure for muteness, to convert its prisoners to martyrdom, to destroy its idols.

So what is my brother searching for by the river beyond the orchard? He is carrying his .22. Muskrats swim in the slower waters late in the fall, but now the tree limbs and twigs are coated in veils of ice. The sky is streaked with blood at dusk. Each shot reverberates as memory across the land.

He used to tell us they were omens, the apples. Each one prefiguring a life. Some with fire blight. Others black rot, codling moths, apple scab, cankers.

Say it is our father wandering once more through the orchard. Snow falling everywhere like arrows.

Field Guide at Noon

This glare on the fallen sweetgum
trunk. The eye of it, the pupil full.
As though to horde the light and let it
burn. And then the leaves: star-shaped,
with pointed lobes, and swaying.
This slow, old dance amid the ancient
smells of loam and rot. To believe
like that: to fall to earth then to twitch
again as though alive. The slow hours
of the birds and their desultory songs:
Here is our soft sleep at noon, our drowsy dreams.
Not as though everything has stopped
but nearly: the way the heart pauses
between beats, lingers. And the wind,
which can barely lift itself from the dirt,
snared in the field's tall grass.
And what of the heat?
It gathers everywhere like a rebuke:
some sweet-lipped god singeing us
with avenging weight. Surely this is
not what we deserve. And yet we do:
to squint at the canker sore that is
our sun. To stand by this fallen
tree that wants to believe it is alive.

Residue

And so the slash pines. The saw-palmetto.
The full-grown deer. Bloated
in heavy summer beside the stream,
the dead heat claiming the last few licks
of water. Green water: murky and congealed
in the moldering skin of days. While the limbs
of the blackjack oak impale the unforgiving sun.
And so the boys: here again to poke
at the deer with a stick. Poke at the beard
of dried blood. Poke at the milk eyes
and the hidden crease between the legs.
Which makes the death flies scatter.
For in death, it seems, the deer is a waxen ghost.
A reliquary. And so: the boys would cut
into the entrails if they knew to read them.
Would carry the severed hooves in their pockets.
For look: the deer's neck is twisted
at that otherworldly angle. And: the smell of death
has transformed the woods into this dim veil.
They love the deer—if love is the rain
that forms in the one gray cloud that drifts
above the stream. Rain that never
brings itself to fall. This stream mud is hardening
and forming cracks in the heat of day.
And so: they do not want to leave the deer.
They sit beside it with their sticks. And they know
they will remember the deer with a lover's
intensity when they are sitting later at the kitchen
table. Or falling asleep at night in their beds.
They will lift their sticks in the mind's eye. Poke.

The Art of Woods

As though some great boot or hand has swept
through the woods. So many trees shorn.
An augury of scattered limbs and dying wood.
And what comes to mind is life crawling from the mud,
from the unformed clay of spring. Like the potter's
workshop: the teeming collection of finished
and unfinished water jugs, storage jars with lids,
cups and saucers, floral vases, stem cups, porridge bowls.
Serving plates painted robin's egg blue, some decorated
with an orange lizard, some with a praying mantis
or a grasshopper, some with blackened hawk's wings.
Or the way the unbaked clay cakes to the boots
on a wet evening weeks after the ice storm.
Watch how the dim welt of twilight throbs
between the trees, bruising the body's ridge.
The handiwork of fallen twigs and leaf meal.
The premonition of willow polypore, hen of the woods,
chanterelle, collybia. See how the tree bends
to make of itself a dead and decaying arch.
Here is gathering night dense as the wood block,
black-gray, suggestive of a face and part of a torso,
solemn and imperial, or perhaps a woman's belly sloped
as though with child. And here are the brush strokes
of dimming goat's rue, wild geraniums, climbing bittersweet.
The raw sex of buds protruding from the moldy wet.
Every configured shadow with a beast's head, talons
or claws formed by the forges of Hephaestus.
Imagine the insistent thump of drums, the sudden rush
of hooves, the goats' heads stuck on stakes,
the surging bonfire flames, the wild whoops and cries.
Or think of the catbird—thief that it is—mewing
like a cat, like the sound Hephaestus heard in his head
when he fell for nine days and nine nights.
Or the time I was a child of maybe seven
and the dining room window reflected back
the living world, and a catbird thumped
into what must have seemed the bright swell of dusk,
raw as a bitten peach—then lay still in the chickweed,

the betony, and the broadleaf straying wild near the house.
The bird's long dark tail a fan brush or mop brush.
The black bill and cap, the chestnut undertail coverts,
the gray emptied eyes. Surely the bird would burrow
at any moment back into the loam and thus return
into the cauldron of mud; but, as I was watching,
it twitched and convulsed like Cassandra,
like a *mal de prophètes*, like Dostoevsky's ecstatic epilepsy.
Then flew off as a mystic to the black woods.

Swamp Dance

The lid lifted again from a jar of formalin
in my grandfather's cellar: the clinging smell
of the oxbow lake. Bats flying out of the cypress
trees. Misshapen wings constructed
from bark and mud. Bodies the size
of a clenched fist. And my grandfather
showing me the shriveled creatures preserved
inside pickle jars: the cavernous ears
and squashed faces, the flesh-wings folded
inward like a shawl. And the final bed
in the back bedroom of my parents' house:
my grandfather like the catfish I saw him drag
once onto the dock: seizing out of the body,
flapping out of the body—until crushed by a boot
on the head. The bats are lolling
up from the swamp like a loosed tongue, listing
in this formaldehyde of air, twitching
until the night's tongue swallows them.

Archaic Light

This must be the beginning
of something: bruised light
cradling the dusk sky
with low-slung clouds
which are themselves the columns
of the world.

Light so dense you can almost
hold it in your hands.

Not like the waterthrush skimming
the rocks, scooping the errant flecks
of sunlight in its beak
as though to build
a nest of it.

Nor like Rilke's
silent friend
of many distances—
breath enlarging all of space.

But childhood light,
browned as a wheat biscuit,
falling into the dead grass at the field's edge.

Trickster light,
like walking out on the lake's ice in winter
until you feel it *begin*
to crack.

Light as ancient and mournful
as the golden lyre.

Light falling, a diary of days
across the junipers
and paper birches, their branches
pointing frail fingers
toward the sky.

Bottomlands Death

Winter: the frozen cracks of ice
along the stream, the portents,
while the brothers are watching
their crucified breaths and speaking
above the tracks of the coyote.
As though the shadow of morning
might suddenly lift the snow
along the ridge and send it floating
down to settle amid the shagbark hickories.
The brothers have been speaking in low voices
about their niece who gave birth that week
to a blind child. The infant was embedded
in her body. The infant was a strange remnant
plucked from an unwilling garden.
The child died in less than an hour,
and that same afternoon the brothers
spotted a dead crow hidden behind
a cedar stump beside their cabin.
The crow studied them with glassy
eyes. The crow tucked its wings
into the snow. The brothers are following
the coyote tracks deep into the woods.
They notice how the front paw prints
are larger than the back. They notice
the coyote scat on the dead leaves.
They carry their rifles on their shoulders,
the same way they plan to carry the coyote
when they come back. They will set it down
beside the cedar stump. They will smear
its blood on the dead crow. They will bury
both in the frozen winter earth.

Black Tar Morning

And so. Everything seeps downhill into these bottomlands.
We study the yellow heads of the prothonotary warblers.
The abandoned crawfish burrows. And yes. The dead
musk turtle half buried in the mud.

So: when this young wife south of the lake miscarried.
And: when this other child is skipping rocks across the slough.
Each rock does not want. Want to be dragged down to its fate
in the alluvium.

This we know: the reeking water fouls the lungs. Or let's say
the tupelos are disfigured. The limbs as black as tar.
While the barred owl is martyring itself in the tangled crook
at midnight. So say: the hen of the woods announces who is dying.

So say: the moon is parasitic. Feeding on the dead waters.
Or: the moon is a great bleached skull above the sweetgums.
Still: no moon is a pale breast. We do not suckle. Look:
this wood stork died.

We pluck one white feather, one black feather. Set them afire.
And still: who is there to read the smoke? And still: the days smolder
and congeal. And yesterday a heron skimmed low across
the waters. Then: the shadow of two crows passed beneath

and through its body. And: the morning fog sags heavily
as a shroud. So say the heat is gathering. The suffocating heat:
gathering. While: the boy watches each stone skip
until it sinks then disappears into the water.

Mud Voice

And then: this voice of the lake.
The alluvial tongue of it. Say egrets.
Say herons. Say storks. This alligator
snapping turtle dragging itself as sucking sound
from the shallows. This stained-green carapace.
And then: the old men with their fishing lines.
Say catfish. Say gar. Say pickerels.
The wrinkled augury of skin. The tongue
of years. And yet. And so. At night
the lovers sneaking down to the lake
to lie in the soft grass. Say mosquito.
Say peeper frog. Say chigger.
Then every story of the feral cat
that becomes the cougar that becomes
the man. And every story of a woman
who sees three crows in a black tupelo
so has a miscarriage. This grief
that is the night air. The white bone
of moon floating above the sweetgum trees.
This black water as a stain. Say no.
Say no. Four children playing
with the lost skin of a cottonmouth.
Two wives on a back porch.
Scowling. The evening sky like a bloodletting.
And somewhere in the distance
a sandhill crane shrieking like it's been gutted.

Alluvium

She wanted to leave. She imagined driving north
past the last sweetbay tree, the last bald cypress.
Maybe the air would grow so cold she couldn't smell it.
She would bring with her one black feather
from a wood stork. A tail of a ground skink.
A dried swamp lily. When her children woke they
would not know that she was gone. *Between here
and there. Between here and there is this road.*
Each night she falls back into bed. Each morning
she rises. Her husband swims in the slough
with the water moccasins. The vertical slits of pupils
watch. She imagines a dead whip scorpion
on the car floor as she drives. The broken-off claw
of a bobcat. The bloodied entrails of a bullfrog
in a mason jar. Her boys take their sticks into the yard
to chase a possum. Look how the creature flees.
Its moon-white face is incorporeal. *The road grows
spectral as an owl amid the trees.* She was born
in the alluvium of this lake. Her children
were born in this alluvium. Her husband drags
a dead doe to the back porch where it summons
another augury of horse flies. Maybe it will snow.
The road will finally end and the sky will fill
with enough frozen white to bury everything.

Late Husband

In her dreams, then, she imagined him as feverish.
He had lost his voice and his skin burned.
They were walking by the lake, and he was trying
to speak, but his voice sounded like a wood duck
or a sandhill crane or a barred owl. Sometimes
she imagined his tongue was floating in the stagnant
waters by the pickerelweed and flowering wapato.
Or that he was swimming with the water moccasins.
Or coiling into the cypress trees drooping with Spanish moss.
And then, when she awoke, she believed she felt the weight
of him beside her, the denseness of swamp mud
in the cloying heat of summer. Moonlight fell
through the windows, and with it came the voices
of cricket frogs. They were feverish at midnight.
Or perhaps she drifted back to sleep, for she imagined
reaching down to feel a wet stream of eggs slipping
from her into the shallow waters around the bed.

Bitter Duration

In *The Sonnets to Orpheus*,
Rilke compares love to a flower
whose name he has forgotten.
                That flower is called *locoweed*.

Imagine the poor cows lured by hunger
to the whorled stalks and the pink buds—
then staggering and collapsing
in the ditch.

While tonight the moonlight is reflected
in this lake we're driving past. The years
moving on with the same lunar tug.

The bleached skull following us
in the shallows, the stars inventing
themselves from heat and memory.

The worms drowning in the soil
each time the drought ends
and the rains fall.

The moon following us
full hearted and fluttering
across the lake.

Accustomed Hour

The day is a body dragged from the congealing waters. She watches from the window.

Imagines that the yellow flag and Spanish moss and swamp lilies are an incantation. Imagines the weak light behind the hornbeams and persimmons claiming the hour.

What she asks of the morning is that a body learn once more to breathe, that the pale skin of day rises from the swamp like an alligator snapping turtle appearing with its plated carapace amid the pickerelweed.

And since her husband and children are still asleep, this is the moment to conjure a life from the clamoring of wood storks, from the sweetgum trees oozing from open wounds the bitter resin.

To imagine the hours rising from the mud, the hours possessed at last in the small light.

Here where the dead form as green muck in the stagnant shallows, where the morning falls gray as ash in the duckweed.

Driving on the Ridge and Seeing Smoke

The world is floating tonight in its bucket.
That's all we are: the wet earth catching the light from stars,
the desiccated moon wanting to commiserate.
Our lives, it seems, are small seeds of light, this geography
of inland and outland, which is another way of saying

we are bones and breath. I imagine the days as cadences—
maybe that's what it means to be growing old.
The boot steps tapping in our sleep,

the wet mud beside the barn where we'll go walking at first light.
We think words will tell it, like a car winding
with its senseless eyes, and all the grass at the road's verge

swaying toward us. Another dark shaft of night. It's not so bad.
We get used to the way it covers the body. Like smoke
rising from a distant chimney down below. This swirl

of tongue reminding us, again, that we are speaking.

Forsaken

He imagines her as the leatherleaf in the woods
behind her farm. The jimsonweed.

The buffalo bur. And nights whenever a train
goes rumbling across her ridge, he thinks of her

as moonlight growing weighty in the belly
of a cloud. Then it is August. The heat gathers itself.

The heat lifts itself and spreads across the prairie fields like oil.
Mornings, now, he works in the fields and imagines

her in her yellow house across the road, imagines her husband
busy with the chickens by the barn, imagines her waking

their young children, kneeling to fasten their buttons,
whispering forsaken secrets in their ears. And if there is fire

at twilight, fire each time the horizon burns into itself
then disappears, he understands that these are auguries and signs.

The wind blowing through the mulberries.
The soil sweating and alive beneath his feet.

Wooing

So this must be a kind of wooing:
the ancient river carrying mud
as its sacred freight. The lowslung stars
and their portent of light. And then
the moon, white as a feather, white as flesh,
white as pale insect larvae or a water moccasin
opening its hypnotic mouth. Like the story
in these parts of a young bride transforming
into an egret on her wedding day, transforming
at the moment her husband is carrying
her across the threshold of their cabin.
Later he would claim he saw it coming:
the stray bit of feather on his lips after he kissed
her neck, his dream of seeing her flying low
above the swamp. All he knows is that suddenly
there is a commotion of wings.
An epileptic writhing. He sees the black legs
and the yellow bill. Sees the nuptial plumes.
This must be a kind of wooing:
the slow catfish with their great bodies
moving in the shallows. Heavy as logs.
The way the moon hides for a moment
behind a gauze of cloud. And the deep
blue fruit of these black tupelos dangling
like testicles. He makes a potion of swamp lilies
and epidendrum. Severs the long neck
of a chicken turtle and smears the blood
on a single white feather his bride left behind.
This must be a kind of wooing: in some dreams
he wades into water as thick as mud or blood,
looking for his bride, and the moon is as pale
as bone, as salt. In other dreams his wife
is thrashing forever in his arms—or flying
above the river then disappearing.

Bright Snake

The heart is the size of a child's fist.
It is a doe's heart, and it is not beating.
And beyond her husband's shoulder—
beyond where he is kneeling by the deer
he dragged up from the bottomlands—
the dusk-covered sun has been stabbed
with a hunting knife and is bleeding
amid the magnolias and sweetbays. And once
in a dream the lake beyond
their cabin was transformed to the bright colors
of a coral snake, and that snake was either
the living flesh or the discarded skin.
Sometimes when her son's asthma strikes,
his chest heaves and his mouth opens
then closes, opens then closes, like a catfish
dragged from the lake and left thrashing
on the shore. Earlier she heard
the rifle exploding from the swamp.
One. Two. Three. Now her husband
wipes the bloody knife against his jeans
then stands. Their son has come out
of the house and walks down to his father.
He steps around the doe with its drooped head
and its exposed chest and belly. The evening
is so warm she almost cannot breathe. And the lake
is shimmering and burning beyond them.

Swamp Lines

She tells herself the rain feels warm
as spit. Warm as twilight burning
into the leaves of the sweetgum trees.
As though the only measure
of a life is how it radiates against
the skin: her father when she was small
slicing off the antlers of a buck,
the dark blood making
of his fingers a lamentation.
Her sisters swimming in the lake:
the brackish waters close
against their naked bodies.
When her son was born she dreamed
one night of wading through the swales
as they were gathering from a heavy rain
into a lake. It was Menses Lake—
while all around her pressed heavy-breasted
night. That summer she and her husband
lay uncovered in the bed,
and on their skin the sweat
would make a seal: skin slick
as a tongue, as a fish slipping
through fingers as they close.
Sometimes she would rise and cross
to the window where she would see
the swamp transform the moonlight
into liquid. A covenant of dark water
and of mud.

Vespers

Dusk light is clinging to the river.
We do not think of this as blood.
The wild buckwheat has opened
its yellow flowers to the heat.
And although the night is gathering—
not as a premonition, not as finality—
the sagebrush will glow incorporeal
beneath the bleached moon.
For there is comfort in remembering,
as though the vesper sparrow—laying
its eggs in the small depression in the ground,
singing its melancholy song at twilight—
will fly against the red sky as a wraith.
This is not the blood light congealing
into clouds. Not the river current moving
slowly as a dream.
We have come here this evening to stand
amid the sagebrush: perhaps a coyote will carry
past us in its jaws a twitching kangaroo rat.
Perhaps a night lizard will drop its tail
as a reliquary across the exposed rock.
We want the flatness of the days to speak
to us amid the locoweed. For the moon
to lift itself above the river like powdered bone.

Prefigured

And so she dreams sometimes of angled sunlight
casting a great blue heron's shadow back
onto the yellow flag and swamp lilies.
Or she grinds up whirligig beetles and water boatmen
for a salve. Or she squeezes four drops
from red elderberries and leaves them
on her sleeping husband's chest. Nothing lives
in the pots she places on their cabin's back porch,
and the weight of her husband against her at night
is the weight of premonition: hoot owls proclaiming
their loneliness to the swamp, chorus frogs
piercing the sky's darkness with prefigured moans.
Some evenings she wades into the noxious water
and rubs her belly with pickerelweed and bladderwort
to make it grow. Once she sees in the distance
an alligator thrashing through shallows toward
a snowy egret—its long legs spindly—and at once
there is a spray and blur of water and a scattering
of feathers. Then the alligator is gone,
and the snowy egret is gone, and she can't decide
whether it flew away or was dragged under.

Field Guide in Winter

I believed, then, you could drown
in wind. You could feel the breath
of it rushing out of the field
like a lung collapsing. Who can say
what bones might be unearthed there?
The clouds that sagged with snow
and the fence post that rattled yet
still clung. To remember that loose
tooth of morning and the frozen
cistern into which a mouse might fall,
or a sparrow, or once a possum whose
face gazed up like a small moon.
The fields were hollow at night
and we lay in bed and listened
to the world being stripped down.
Your breaths in the bunk bed above
me were small as the icicles
clinging to the eaves. In my dreams
the field spread out before us like a
strange salt sea, but later, when
you were gone, it evaporated into
snow, and the wind whipped
around me so I couldn't breathe.

Ladder Without Rungs

And so the years pass. And the old ones who are left by the river feel the dull sky above the tupelos turning increasingly to stone.

The *Volvaria* and the *Laccaria* are whispering from the woods.

The old women are standing on their porches trying to listen.

The old men are gutting the catfish they caught this evening in the unmoving waters near the bridge.

And look: the small branches of the black willows by the elder's house are trembling like an occultation, and the running water beyond the cemetery sounds almost but not quite like the voices of children playing.

And late tonight the moon turns to bone above the ridge, and in their dreams the old ones who are left are *climbing*   *climbing*

to the unspeakable, which is what the hoot owl imagines in its lonely patient cry, which I hear through the screen mesh of my window while darkness presses its black tongue against the trees.

Carapace

Say from these windows. Say the swamp.
The sweetgums leaning into the infinite.
The tupelos. And here: this old woman.
Let's say she is dying. Let's say this bed
on which she lies is made of auguries.
And then: the moon is salt tonight, a pale
hand. And what of the peeper frogs and bullfrogs?
And then her family peering in the doorway,
or sitting in a chair or on the corner
of the bed. And what sound is this the wind
makes in the bottomlands? Washing across
the pickerelweed and swamp lilies.
Entering the screen mesh. Then morning
like a tired bowl of light. The heat
the memory of being born: the child
as alluvium, as river mud. A life like that.
Say she is swimming in the brackish waters.
Say she is an ancient turtle with the green
muck clinging to her carapace. Isn't
someone there to hold her hand?
Look: a great blue heron has landed
in the slow-moving river. And: the white
feathers of the egret when it stirs
its wings. Say each breath the old woman
manages. Say being a child again
and diving deep into the water, feeling
the reeds pressing against the body.
Say the lungs now dense with moss
and yellow flag. Remembering them
as tall once as she was.

Possum Nocturne

The boy found a possum skull
beside a tulip tree. A dead tree.
There were wood blewits,
Tricholoma and inky caps
thriving near the fallen limbs,
which stank and rotted.
The skull itself was bleached
and heavy, as though the rows
of teeth remembered insects,
robins' eggs, and carrion. At night
he held the skull against his chest
and dreamed that the possum
followed him through the woods,
its face pale and otherworldly.
Other times he imagined leaving
the skull by the upright stone
of his father's grave. The skull
would watch the moon drifting
above the dogwood and hickories.
The wind would wail through the teeth.
And the boy, awakening in bed,
would cross to the window and listen.

Doug Ramspeck is the author of *Black Tupelo Country*, which received the 2007 John Ciardi Prize for poetry, and is published by BkMk Press. He is also the author of *Where We Come From* (March Street Press). In 2009 he was awarded an Ohio Arts Council Individual Excellence Award. Ramspeck directs the Writing Center and teaches at The Ohio State University at Lima. He lives with his wife, Beth, and their daughter, Lee.

Also from NorthShore Press:

The Cormorant Hunter's Wife, by Joan Kane
poetry, 80 pages, $19.00

Between Fire and Water, Ice and Sky, by Gretchen Diemer
poetry, 88 pages with CD, $18.00

Cartography of Water, by Mike Burwell
poetry, 88 pages with CD, $16.00